Mastering Blazor WebAssembly Crash Course

Create High-Performance Web UIs with C#! Master the Essentials in 7 Days and Understand Blazor's Architecture and Beyond!

By

Andrew M. Jones

Table of contents

INTRODUCTION... **5**

**Blazor WebAssembly Crash Course: Unleash the
Power of C# for Blazing-Fast Web UIs (Even if
You're New!)**...**5**

Chapter 1... **12**

Introduction to Blazor WebAssembly.....................**12**

**Limitations of Traditional JavaScript Frameworks
and the Blazor WebAssembly Alternative**..............**21**

**Introducing Blazor WebAssembly: A Game Changer
in Web Development**...............................**29**

Benefits of Using C# for Web Development............. **34**

Chapter 2... **41**

Getting Started with Blazor WebAssembly..............**41**

Understanding the Blazor Project Structure........... **48**

**Creating Your First Blazor WebAssembly
Application**.. **54**

Chapter 3... **61**

**Introduction to Razor Syntax: HTML with C# Magic
61**

Creating Basic Blazor Components: The Building
Blocks...68

Data Binding: Connecting Your UI to C# Code........76

Chapter 4..84

User Interactions and Event Handling.....................84

Handling Events Effectively: Buttons, Forms, and
More..93

Understanding Cascading Parameters and Event
Bubbling in Blazor...103

Chapter 5..112

Styling Your Blazor Applications with CSS............112

Component-Level and Global Styling Options.......118

Applying Bootstrap or Other CSS Frameworks.... 124

Chapter 6..130

Working with Data in Blazor WebAssembly...........131

Handling API Responses and Displaying Data.......140

Introduction to Dependency Injection for Data
Services in Blazor WebAssembly............................150

Chapter 7..157

State Management in Blazor Applications............157

Implementing Application State with Blazor State

Management Library... 167

Sharing State Between Components Effectively.....174

Chapter 8..182

Persisting Data in Blazor WebAssembly.................. 182

Integrating Blazor with IndexedDB for Persistent

Storage... 188

Part I:..196

Blazor WebAssembly Fundamentals...................... 196

Chapter 9:...203

Optimizing and Deploying Blazor WebAssembly

Apps.. 204

Chapter 10:...209

Deployment Options for Blazor WebAssembly

Applications..211

Part II:.. 217

Advanced Topics.. 217

Chapter 11:...217

Beyond the Basics: Advanced Blazor Techniques.. 217

Chapter 12:...225

Authentication and Authorization in Blazor...........226

Chapter 13:...233

Debugging and Troubleshooting Blazor
WebAssembly...235

Part III:...235

Community and Resources...............................235

Chapter 14:...241

Exploring the Blazor Documentation and Learning
Resources...241

Conclusion...247

Appendix...252

A: Glossary of Terms...256

INTRODUCTION

Blazor WebAssembly Crash Course: Unleash the Power of C# for Blazing-Fast Web UIs (Even if You're New!)

Blazor WebAssembly is a revolutionary framework that allows you to build interactive web UIs using C# instead of JavaScript. It's part of the .NET ecosystem, meaning you can leverage your existing C# knowledge to create web applications.

Getting Started

To begin, you'll need the .NET SDK installed. Create a new Blazor WebAssembly app using the following command:

```bash
Bash

dotnet new blazorwasm -o MyBlazorApp
```

This creates a new directory named MyBlazorApp containing your Blazor project.

Understanding Blazor Components

Blazor applications are built using components. These are reusable pieces of UI with their own logic. Let's create a simple component:

```csharp
C#

// Counter.razor
<h1>Counter</h1>
<p>Current count: @currentCount</p>
<button class="btn btn-primary"
@onclick="IncrementCount">Click me</button>

@code {
```

```
private int currentCount = 0;

private void IncrementCount()
{

    currentCount++;



}
}
```

This component displays a counter and a button.
Clicking the button increments the count.

Data Binding

Blazor supports two-way data binding, which means changes in the UI are automatically reflected in your C# code and vice versa. Consider this example:

```
C#
// InputForm.razor
<input type="text" @bind-value="Name" />
<p>Hello, @Name!</p>

@code {
    public string Name { get; set; }
}
```

Typing in the input box updates the Name property, and changes to Name are reflected in the input.

Building Interactive UIs

Blazor provides rich features for building interactive UIs. You can handle events, create custom components,

9

and manage application state using techniques like state management libraries. Here's an example of a basic form with validation:

```csharp
// ContactForm.razor
<EditForm Model="@contact" OnValidSubmit="HandleSubmit">
    <InputText @bind-Value="contact.Name" />
    <InputText @bind-Value="contact.Email" />
    <ValidationSummary />
    <button type="submit">Submit</button>
</EditForm>

@code {
    private Contact contact = new Contact();

    private void HandleSubmit()
    {
        // Handle form submission
    }
```

Conclusion

This crash course has introduced you to the basics of Blazor WebAssembly. You've learned how to create components, bind data, and build interactive UIs. To master Blazor, explore topics like dependency injection, routing, and state management in more detail.

Additional Tips

- **Leverage C# features:** Use LINQ, async/await, and other C# constructs to write efficient code.
- **Utilize Blazor components:** The Blazor component model promotes code reusability.
- **Explore community resources:** There's a thriving Blazor community with plenty of resources and libraries.

- **Practice regularly:** Build small projects to solidify your understanding.

By following these guidelines and delving deeper into Blazor's capabilities, you can create impressive web applications with unmatched performance and developer experience.

Would you like to dive deeper into a specific aspect of Blazor WebAssembly, such as data binding, state management, or deployment?

Chapter 1

Introduction to Blazor WebAssembly

Introduction to Blazor WebAssembly

Blazor WebAssembly is a .NET framework for building interactive web UIs using C# instead of JavaScript. It runs client-side in the browser, offering a full-stack development experience with C#.

Core Concepts

- **Components**: The building blocks of Blazor apps, combining HTML, CSS, and C# code into reusable units.
- **Razor Syntax**: A syntax for embedding C# code within HTML, enabling dynamic UI generation.
- **Data Binding**: Seamlessly connecting C# properties to UI elements for automatic updates.
- **Lifecycle Methods**: Methods that are called at different stages of a component's lifecycle.
- **Routing**: Navigating between different pages or views in a Blazor app.

Creating a Basic Blazor App

To start, create a new Blazor WebAssembly project using the .NET CLI:

```bash
Bash

dotnet new blazorwasm -o MyBlazorApp
```

Building Your First Component

Replace the contents of Pages/Counter.razor with the following:

```csharp
C#

<h1>Counter</h1>

<p>Current count: @currentCount</p>

<button class="btn btn-primary"
@onclick="IncrementCount">Click me</button>


@code {

    private int currentCount = 0;
```

```
private void IncrementCount()

{

    currentCount++;
```

```
    }

}
```

This component displays a counter and a button.
Clicking the button increments the count.

Data Binding

Blazor supports two-way data binding, making it easy to synchronize data between the UI and C# code:

```csharp
<input type="text" @bind-value="Name" />

<p>Hello, @Name!</p>


@code {

    public string Name { get; set; }

}
```

Any changes made in the input field will be reflected in the Name property, and vice versa.

Handling Events

Blazor simplifies event handling with the `@onclick` attribute:

```csharp
C#
```

```
<button @onclick="HandleButtonClick">Click me</button>


@code {

    private void HandleButtonClick()

    {

        // Your event handler logic here

    }

}
```

Routing

Blazor supports routing to create single-page applications (SPAs):

```C#
<Router AppAssembly="@typeof(Program).Assembly">
    <Route Path="/" Component="{typeof(Index)}" />

    <Route Path="/counter" Component="{typeof(Counter)}" />

    <Route Path="/fetchdata" Component="{typeof(FetchData)}" />
</Router>
```

This defines routes for different pages in your application.

Additional Tips

- **Leverage C# features:** Use LINQ, async/await, and other C# constructs for efficient code.
- **Component reusability:** Create reusable components to improve code organization.
- **State management:** Consider using state management libraries for complex applications.
- **Performance optimization:** Optimize your Blazor app for fast rendering and responsiveness.
- **Debugging:** Use browser developer tools and Blazor's debugging features to troubleshoot issues.

Conclusion

This introduction provides a solid foundation for building Blazor WebAssembly applications. By understanding components, data binding, events, and routing, you can create interactive and dynamic web experiences.

To delve deeper, explore topics like:

19

- Dependency injection
- Lifecycle methods
- Forms and validation
- JavaScript interop
- Deployment options

Would you like to explore any of these topics in more detail?

Limitations of Traditional JavaScript Frameworks and the Blazor WebAssembly Alternative

Limitations of Traditional JavaScript Frameworks and the Blazor WebAssembly Alternative

The Challenges of JavaScript Frameworks

JavaScript frameworks have been the cornerstone of web development for years, but they come with inherent limitations:

- **Steep Learning Curve:** Mastering complex JavaScript syntax, ecosystem, and tooling can be time-consuming.
- **Developer Experience:** Debugging JavaScript code can be challenging, and the lack of strong type systems can lead to runtime errors.
- **Performance Overhead:** Virtual DOM diffing and complex state management can impact performance.
- **Tooling Complexity:** Managing multiple build tools, package managers, and transpilers can be overwhelming.

Blazor WebAssembly: A Fresh Perspective

Blazor WebAssembly offers a compelling alternative to traditional JavaScript frameworks by leveraging C# and .NET:

- **Developer Productivity:** C# is a strongly typed language with rich tooling, leading to faster development and fewer errors.
- **Shared Codebase:** Write business logic in C# and share it between server-side and client-side code.
- **Performance:** Blazor compiles to WebAssembly, resulting in high performance and efficient execution.
- **Strong Ecosystem:** Benefit from the mature .NET ecosystem, including libraries, tools, and community support.

Code Example: Comparing JavaScript and Blazor

JavaScript (React):

```JavaScript

```

```jsx
import React, { useState } from 'react';

function Counter() {

  const [count, setCount] = useState(0);

  return (

    <div>

      <p>You clicked {count} times</p>

      <button onClick={() => setCount(count + 1)}>

        Click me

      </button>

    </div>
```

```
);

}
```

Blazor:

```C#
```

```
@page "/counter"



<h3>Counter</h3>



<p>Current count: @currentCount</p>



<button class="btn btn-primary"
@onclick="IncrementCount">Click me</button>
```

24

```
@code {

    private int currentCount



= 0;


    private void IncrementCount()

    {

        currentCount++;
```

As shown, the Blazor code is more concise and readable due to C# syntax and direct DOM manipulation.

Key Advantages of Blazor WebAssembly

* **Rapid Development:** Leverage C# productivity and .NET tooling.

* **Shared Code:** Reuse business logic across server and client.

* **Improved Performance:** Benefit from WebAssembly's efficiency.

* **Strong Typing:** Reduce runtime errors and improve code quality.

* **Rich Ecosystem:** Access to .NET libraries and frameworks.

26

When to Choose Blazor WebAssembly

While Blazor WebAssembly is a powerful tool, it's essential to consider the right use cases:

- **Complex business logic:** Blazor's C# backend is ideal for handling complex calculations and data processing.
- **Existing .NET investments:** If you have a .NET backend, reusing code with Blazor is efficient.
- **High performance:** Blazor's WebAssembly compilation provides excellent performance.
- **Developer preference:** If your team prefers C# over JavaScript, Blazor is a strong option.

Conclusion

Blazor WebAssembly offers a compelling alternative to traditional JavaScript frameworks by addressing common pain points. Its combination of C# productivity, performance, and shared codebase makes it a compelling choice for many web development projects. However,

it's essential to evaluate the specific requirements of your
application before making a decision.

Would you like to delve deeper into specific Blazor
features or compare it to other JavaScript
frameworks?

Introducing Blazor WebAssembly: A Game Changer in Web Development

Introducing Blazor WebAssembly: A Game Changer in
Web Development

Blazor WebAssembly is a revolutionary framework that
empowers developers to build interactive web UIs using
C# instead of JavaScript. By running client-side in the
browser, it offers a full-stack development experience
with the .NET ecosystem.

Breaking Free from JavaScript

Traditional web development heavily relies on JavaScript, often leading to complex projects with potential performance and maintainability issues. Blazor WebAssembly addresses these challenges by providing:

- **C# Development:** Leverage your existing C# skills to build web applications.
- **Improved Performance:** Direct compilation to WebAssembly results in efficient code execution.
- **Rich Ecosystem:** Benefit from the vast .NET ecosystem, including libraries, tools, and community support.
- **Shared Codebase:** Potentially share code between server-side and client-side logic.

Core Concepts

- **Components:** Reusable building blocks of Blazor applications, combining HTML, CSS, and C# code.
- **Razor Syntax:** A syntax for embedding C# code within HTML templates.

29

- **Data Binding**: Seamlessly connect C# properties to UI elements for automatic updates.
- **Lifecycle Methods**: Methods invoked at different stages of a component's lifecycle### Building Your First Blazor App To start, create a new Blazor WebAssembly project using the .NET CLI:

```bash
dotnet new blazorwasm -o MyBlazorApp
```

Replace the contents of Pages/Index.razor with:

```csharp
<h1>Hello, world!</h1>
```

```
<button class="btn btn-primary"
@onclick="IncrementCount">Click me</button>
```

```
<p>You clicked @currentCount times</p>


@code {

    private int currentCount = 0;


    private void IncrementCount()

    {

        currentCount++;

    }

}
```

This creates a simple counter component.

Data Binding

Blazor excels at data binding, keeping UI and C# code in sync:

```C#
<input type="text" @bind-value="Name" />

<p>Hello, @Name!</p>


@code {

    public string Name { get; set; }

}
```

Changes in the input are reflected in the **Name** property and vice versa.

Conclusion

Blazor WebAssembly is a game-changer for web development, offering a fresh approach with C#. Its performance, developer experience, and integration with .NET make it a compelling choice for modern web applications.

Would you like to delve deeper into specific Blazor features, such as routing, component lifecycle, or state management?

Benefits of Using C# for Web Development

Benefits of Using C# for Web Development

C# has traditionally been a strong language for backend development, but with the advent of Blazor, its role in web development has expanded significantly. Let's explore the key benefits of using C# for web development.

Leveraging a Mature Language

- **Strong Typing:** C# is a statically typed language, which helps catch potential errors at compile time, improving code reliability.
- **Object-Oriented Programming (OOP):** C#'s robust OOP support promotes code reusability, maintainability, and scalability.
- **Rich Standard Library:** The .NET Framework provides a comprehensive set of classes and methods for various tasks, accelerating development.

Enhanced Developer Productivity

- **Familiar Syntax:** If you're already a C# developer, transitioning to web development with Blazor is seamless.
- **Integrated Development Environment (IDE):** Visual Studio offers powerful features for debugging, refactoring, and code completion.

- **Rapid Development:** Blazor's component-based architecture and hot reload capabilities boost development speed.

Improved Application Performance

- **Ahead-of-Time (AOT) Compilation:** Blazor WebAssembly compiles C# code to WebAssembly, resulting in faster application startup and execution.
- **Garbage Collection:** C#'s efficient garbage collector manages memory automatically, preventing performance issues.
- **Asynchronous Programming:** C# supports asynchronous programming with `async` and `await`, enabling responsive user interfaces.

Building Robust and Scalable Applications

- **Cross-Platform Development:** C# can be used to build web, desktop, and mobile applications, sharing code across platforms.
- **Cloud Integration:** .NET provides seamless integration with cloud platforms like Azure, AWS, and GCP.
- **Security:** C# and .NET offer strong security features to protect applications from vulnerabilities.

Code Example: Demonstrating C# Power

```csharp
C#

@page "/counter"




<h3>Counter</h3>




<p>Current count: @currentCount</p>
```

```
<button class="btn btn-primary"
@onclick="IncrementCount">Click me</button>


@code {

private int currentCount


= 0;


private void IncrementCount()

{

currentCount++;
```

}

This simple Blazor component showcases C# syntax within Razor syntax, demonstrating how easily you can combine C# logic with HTML.

Conclusion

C# offers a compelling proposition for web development. Its maturity, performance, and developer productivity advantages make it a strong contender for building modern web applications. By combining the power of C# with the flexibility of Blazor, developers can create robust, scalable, and high-performing web experiences.

Would you like to explore specific use cases for C# in web development, or delve deeper into performance optimization techniques?

Chapter 2

Getting Started with Blazor WebAssembly

Getting Started with Blazor WebAssembly

Setting Up Your Environment

Before diving into Blazor, ensure you have the following:

- .NET SDK: Download and install the latest .NET SDK from https://dotnet.microsoft.com/download.
- A code editor or IDE: Visual Studio, Visual Studio Code, or JetBrains Rider are popular choices.

Creating Your First Blazor WebAssembly App

Open a terminal or command prompt and navigate to the desired directory. Create a new Blazor WebAssembly project using the following command:

```bash
dotnet new blazorwasm -o MyBlazorApp
```

Replace MyBlazorApp with your desired project name.

Understanding the Project Structure

The generated project contains the following key folders:

- **wwwroot:** Static files like CSS, JavaScript, and images.
- **Pages:** Contains Razor components representing different pages of your application.
- **Shared:** Shared code accessible from both client and server (for Blazor Hybrid).
- **Components:** Custom components for reusable UI elements.

Building Your First Component

Let's create a simple counter component. Open `Pages/Counter.razor` and replace the content with:

```C#
<h1>Counter</h1>

<p>Current count: @currentCount</p>

<button class="btn btn-primary"
@onclick="IncrementCount">Click me</button>


@code {

    private int currentCount = 0;


    private void IncrementCount()

    {

        currentCount++;
```

```

        }

    }
```

This code defines a component with a counter and a button. The `@onclick` attribute binds the button click to the `IncrementCount` method.

Data Binding

Blazor excels at data binding, connecting UI elements to C# properties:

```
C#
```

```
<input type="text" @bind-value="Name" />

<p>Hello, @Name!</p>


@code {

    public string Name { get; set; }

}
```

Any changes made in the input field will be reflected in the Name property, and vice versa.

Running Your Blazor App

To run the application, navigate to the project directory in your terminal and execute:

```bash
Bash

dotnet run
```

This will start the development server, and you can access your application in the browser at http://localhost:5000.

Key Points to Remember

- **Component-Based Architecture**: Blazor applications are built using reusable components.
- **Razor Syntax**: Combines HTML with C# code for declarative UI creation.
- **Data Binding**: Simplifies data synchronization between UI and C# code.
- **Lifecycle Methods**: Manage component behavior at different stages (e.g., OnInitialized, OnParametersSet).
- **Dependency Injection**: Use built-in dependency injection for managing services.
- **Routing**: Navigate between different pages using Blazor's routing system.

Additional Tips

- **Leverage C# Features:** Take advantage of LINQ, async/await, and other C# language features.
- **Use Blazor Components:** Create custom components for reusable UI elements.
- **Explore State Management:** Consider using state management libraries for complex applications.
- **Optimize Performance:** Implement performance best practices for smooth user experiences.
- **Debugging:** Use browser developer tools and Blazor's debugging features to troubleshoot issues.

By following these steps and exploring the Blazor documentation, you'll be well-equipped to build impressive web applications using C#.

Would you like to delve deeper into a specific aspect of Blazor, such as routing, state management, or data fetching?

Understanding the Blazor Project Structure

Understanding the Blazor Project Structure

Overview

A typical Blazor WebAssembly project is organized into several key directories and files. Understanding this structure is crucial for efficient development and maintenance.

Core Directories

- **wwwroot:** Contains static assets such as CSS, JavaScript, images, and index.html.

- **Pages:** Houses Razor components that represent individual pages or views of your application.
- **Shared:** Shared code accessible from both client and server (for Blazor Hybrid).
- **Components:** Custom components for reusable UI elements.

Additional Directories (Optional)

- **Data:** Used to store data access logic or models.
- **Services:** For defining application services.
- **Models:** For defining data models.

Key Files

- **Program.cs:** Application entry point and dependency injection configuration.
- **appsettings.json:** Configuration settings for the application.

Breakdown

- **wwwroot:** This directory holds static resources that are directly served to the client.

  a. **index.html:** The main HTML file that loads the Blazor application.

  b. **css:** Contains stylesheets for your application.

  c. **js:** Contains JavaScript files (though less common in Blazor).

  d. **images:** Stores images used in your application.

- **Pages:** This directory houses Razor components, which are the building blocks of your Blazor UI. Each Razor file (.razor) represents a page or a reusable component.

  a. **Index.razor:** The default page when the application starts.

  b. **Counter.razor:** A common example component included in new Blazor projects.

  c. **FetchData.razor:** Another example component for fetching data.

- **Shared:** This directory is for code shared between the client and server in Blazor Hybrid applications. It's often used for data models or utility classes.
- **Components:** Used to organize custom components for reusability. This is optional but recommended for larger projects.

Example Project Structure

```
MyBlazorApp/
├── wwwroot/
│   ├── index.html
│   ├── css/
│   ├── js/
│   └── images/
├── Pages/
│   ├── Counter.razor
│   ├── FetchData.razor
│   └── Index.razor
├── Shared/
```

```
│   ├── NavMenu.razor
│   └── MainLayout.razor
├── Components/
│   ├── MyCustomComponent.razor
├── Program.cs
├── appsettings.json
└── ... other project files
```

Best Practices

- **Organize code effectively**: Use folders and subfolders to structure your project logically.
- **Leverage components**: Create reusable components for better code maintainability.
- **Utilize shared code**: Share code between client and server when applicable.
- **Keep wwwroot clean**: Avoid unnecessary files in the wwwroot directory.

By understanding this structure, you can efficiently organize your Blazor projects and improve code maintainability.

Would you like to dive deeper into a specific aspect of Blazor project structure or explore other related topics?

Creating Your First Blazor WebAssembly Application

Creating Your First Blazor WebAssembly Application

Prerequisites

Before diving into Blazor, ensure you have the following:

- **.NET SDK:** Download and install the latest .NET SDK from https://dotnet.microsoft.com/download.
- **A code editor or IDE:** Visual Studio, Visual Studio Code, or JetBrains Rider are popular choices.

Creating a New Blazor WebAssembly Project

1. Open a terminal or command prompt.
2. Navigate to the desired directory.
3. Create a new Blazor WebAssembly project:
4. Bash

```
dotnet new blazorwasm -o MyBlazorApp
```

5.
6. Replace MyBlazorApp with your desired project name.

Understanding the Project Structure

The generated project contains the following key folders:

- **wwwroot:** Static files like CSS, JavaScript, and images.
- **Pages:** Contains Razor components representing different pages of your application.
- **Shared:** Shared code accessible from both client and server (for Blazor Hybrid).
- **Components:** Custom components for reusable UI elements.

Building Your First Component

Let's create a simple counter component. Open Pages/Counter.razor and replace the content with:

```
C#
```

`<h1>Counter</h1>`

`<p>Current count: @currentCount</p>`

`<button class="btn btn-primary"
@onclick="IncrementCount">Click me</button>`

```
@code {

    private int currentCount = 0;


    private void IncrementCount()

    {

        currentCount++;



    }

}
```

This code defines a component with a counter and a button. The @onclick attribute binds the button click to the IncrementCount method.

Running Your Blazor App

To run the application, navigate to the project directory in your terminal and execute:

```bash
Bash

dotnet run
```

This will start the development server, and you can access your application in the browser at http://localhost:5000.

Key Components of a Blazor App

* **Razor Components:** These are the building blocks of Blazor apps, combining HTML, CSS, and C# code into reusable units.

* **Component Lifecycle:** Blazor components have lifecycle methods like `OnInitialized`, `OnParametersSet`, and `OnAfterRender` for managing component behavior.

- **Data Binding:** Blazor supports two-way data binding, allowing seamless synchronization between UI elements and C# properties.
- **Routing:** Navigate between different pages using Blazor's routing system.
- **Dependency Injection:** Use built-in dependency injection to manage services and dependencies.

Additional Tips

- **Leverage C# Features:** Take advantage of LINQ, async/await, and other C# language features for efficient code.
- **Utilize Blazor Components:** Create reusable components for better code organization and maintainability.
- **Explore State Management:** Consider using state management libraries for complex applications.

- **Optimize Performance:** Implement performance best practices to ensure a smooth user experience.
- **Debugging:** Use browser developer tools and Blazor's debugging features to troubleshoot issues.

By following these steps and exploring the Blazor documentation, you've laid the foundation for building robust and interactive web applications using C#.

Would you like to delve deeper into a specific aspect of Blazor, such as routing, state management, or data fetching?

Chapter 3

Introduction to Razor Syntax: HTML with C# Magic

Introduction to Razor Syntax: HTML with C# Magic

Razor syntax is a powerful combination of HTML and C# that forms the foundation of Blazor applications. It allows you to seamlessly blend markup and code, creating dynamic and interactive user interfaces.

Basic Razor Syntax

A Razor file typically has a `.razor` extension and consists of two main sections:

- **HTML markup:** Standard HTML elements and attributes.
- **C# code:** Encoded within @ symbols.

Example:

```C#
```
<h1>Hello, World!</h1>

<p>The current time is: @DateTime.Now</p>

In this example:

- `<h1>Hello, World!</h1>` is standard HTML.
- `@DateTime.Now` is C# code embedded within the HTML.

Code Blocks

For larger blocks of C# code, you can use code blocks:

```C#
@code {

    private int count = 0;


    private void IncrementCount()

    {

        count++;

    }

}
```

Expressions

You can embed C# expressions directly within HTML using @:

```C#
<p>The answer is: @(42 + 1)</p>
```

Statements

While expressions are evaluated and their result is inserted into the output, statements are executed for their side effects. You can use statements within @:

```C#
@if (condition)
{
```

```
    <p>The condition is true</p>
}
else
{
    <p>The condition is false</p>
}
```

Loops

Razor supports `@for` and `@foreach` loops:

```
C#
<ul>
    @foreach (var item in items)
    {
        <li>@item</li>
    }
```

```
</ul>
```

Attributes

You can bind C# values to HTML attributes:

```C#
<img src="@ImageUrl" alt="Image" />
```

Event Handling

Razor allows you to handle events using @onclick, @onchange, and other event handlers:

```C#
<button @onclick="IncrementCount">Click me</button>
```

```
@code {

    private int count = 0;


    private void IncrementCount()

    {

      count++;

    }

}
```

Razor Directives

Razor directives provide additional control over the
compilation process:

- @page: Defines a page component.
- @inherits: Specifies a base class for a
  component.
- @layout: Sets the layout for a page.

Best Practices

- Use clear and concise code.
- Format your Razor code consistently.
- Leverage C# features for efficient logic.
- Test your Razor components thoroughly.

By mastering Razor syntax, you can create dynamic and interactive user interfaces with ease. It's a powerful tool that empowers you to build complex web applications using C#.

Would you like to dive deeper into a specific aspect of Razor syntax, such as data binding or component lifecycle methods?

Creating Basic Blazor Components: The Building Blocks

Creating Basic Blazor Components: The Building Blocks

Blazor components are the fundamental building blocks for constructing interactive web UIs. They encapsulate UI logic, rendering, and state management within a single unit.

Understanding Components

A Blazor component is essentially a Razor file with a .razor extension. It combines HTML, CSS, and C# code to create reusable UI elements. Components can be nested to build complex UIs, and they can be shared across different parts of your application.

Creating a Simple Component

Let's create a basic component to display a greeting:

```C#
```

// Greeting.razor

<h1>Hello, @Name!</h1>

```
@code {

    [Parameter]

    public string Name { get; set; }

}
```

This component defines a Name parameter that can be passed from the parent component.

Rendering Components

To use this component, you would typically place it within another component or page:

```C#
// Index.razor
```

```
<Greeting Name="World" />
```

Component Lifecycle

Blazor components have a lifecycle with various methods called at different stages:

- **OnInitialized**: Called after the component is first rendered.
- **OnParametersSet**: Called when parameters passed to the component change.
- **OnAfterRender**: Called after the component has been rendered to the DOM.

```C#
@code {

    private int count = 0;


    protected override void OnInitialized()

    {

        count = 10; // Initialize count on component creation

    }
```

}

Component Parameters

You can pass data to components using parameters. The [Parameter] attribute marks a property as a component parameter:

```csharp
C#
```

```csharp
// Counter.razor

<p>Current count: @count</p>

<button class="btn btn-primary"
@onclick="IncrementCount">Click me</button>


@code {

    [Parameter]

    public int InitialCount { get; set; } = 0;
```

```
private


int count = 0;

    protected override void OnInitialized()

    {

        count = InitialCount;

    }


    private void IncrementCount()

    {

        count++;

    }

}
```

Child Components

Components can be nested to create hierarchical UI structures. The parent component can pass data to child components using parameters:

```csharp
C#
```

```csharp
// ParentComponent.razor

<ChildComponent Value="42" />


// ChildComponent.razor

<p>Received value: @Value</p>


@code {

    [Parameter]

    public int Value { get; set; }

}
```

Best Practices

- Keep components focused and reusable.
- Use clear and meaningful names for components and parameters.
- Leverage component lifecycle methods effectively.
- Consider using dependency injection for managing services.
- Test your components thoroughly.

By understanding these fundamentals, you can create well-structured and maintainable Blazor applications.

Would you like to delve deeper into a specific aspect of component creation, such as component rendering, state management, or component interaction?

Data Binding: Connecting Your UI to C# Code

Data Binding: Connecting Your UI to C# Code

Data binding is a cornerstone of modern UI development, and Blazor excels in this area. It allows you to seamlessly connect your UI elements to C# properties, ensuring that changes in one are reflected in the other.

One-Way Binding

One-way binding flows data from a C# property to the UI. Any changes made in the C# code will be reflected in the UI, but changes in the UI won't affect the C# property.

```
C#
```

```
<p>Hello, @Name!</p>
```

73

```
@code {

    public string Name = "World";

}
```

In this example, the value of `Name` from the C# code is
displayed in the UI. If `Name` is changed in the C# code,
the UI will update automatically.

Two-Way Binding

Two-way binding creates a bidirectional connection
between the UI and C# code. Changes made in either
direction are reflected in the other.

```C#
<input type="text" @bind-value="Name" />

<p>Hello, @Name!</p>
```

```
@code {

    public string Name { get; set; } = "World";

}
```

Here, the `@bind-value` syntax establishes two-way binding between the `input` element and the `Name` property. Any changes in the input field will update the `Name` property, and vice versa.

Binding to Collections

Blazor supports binding to collections like arrays and lists:

```C#
@foreach (var item in Items)

    {

        <p>@item</p>
```

```
}
```

```
@code {

    public List<string> Items = new() { "Item 1", "Item
2", "Item 3" };

}
```

Binding to Forms

Blazor simplifies form handling with built-in data
binding:

```C#
<EditForm Model="@person"
OnValidSubmit="HandleSubmit">

    <InputText @bind-Value="person.Name" />
```

```razor
<InputText @bind-Value="person.Email" />

<button type="submit">Submit</button>

</EditForm>


@code {

    public Person Person { get; set; } = new Person();


    private void HandleSubmit()

    {

        // Handle form submission

    }


    public class Person

    {
```

```csharp
    public string Name { get; set; }

    public string Email { get; set; }

    }

}
```

Binding to Events

You can bind C# methods to UI events using the `@onclick`, `@onchange`, and other event handlers:

```csharp
C#
```

```
<button @onclick="IncrementCount">Click
me</button>


@code {

    private int count = 0;
```

```
private void IncrementCount()

{

    count++;

}

}
```

Best Practices

- Use clear and descriptive property names.
- Validate user input to prevent invalid data.
- Consider using [Parameter] for passing data to components.
- Optimize data binding performance for large datasets.
- Explore advanced binding scenarios like @bind:event for custom event handling.

By effectively utilizing data binding, you can create
dynamic and responsive Blazor applications that
seamlessly connect user interactions with underlying
data.

Would you like to explore advanced data binding
techniques or learn about specific use cases?

Chapter 4

User Interactions and Event Handling

User Interactions and Event Handling in Blazor

Blazor provides a streamlined approach to handling user
interactions, making it easy to create dynamic and
responsive web applications.

Basic Event Handling

The most common way to handle user interactions is through event handlers. Blazor offers a declarative syntax for attaching event handlers to HTML elements:

```csharp
C#

<button @onclick="IncrementCount">Click me</button>


@code {

    private int count = 0;


    private void IncrementCount()

    {

        count++;

    }

}
```

In this example, clicking the button triggers the IncrementCount method.

Event Arguments

For more complex scenarios, you might need access to event arguments. You can achieve this by using the EventArgs parameter:

```
C#
```

```
<input type="text" @oninput="HandleInputChange" />

@code {
    private string inputValue = "";


    private void HandleInputChange(ChangeEventArgs
args)
```

```csharp
    {

        inputValue = args.Value.ToString();

    }

}
```

The ChangeEventArgs object provides information about the event, such as the value of the input element.

Custom Events

Blazor allows you to create custom events and handle them within your components:

```csharp
C#
```

```
<CustomButton OnClick="HandleButtonClick" />
```

@code {

```csharp
private void HandleButtonClick()

{

    // Handle button click

}

}
```

C#

```csharp
// CustomButton.razor

<button @onclick="() => OnClick?.Invoke()">Click
me</button>


[Parameter]

public EventCallback<MouseEventArgs> OnClick { get;
set; }
```

This example defines a custom button component that raises a custom OnClick event. The parent component can subscribe to this event and handle it accordingly.

Event Propagation

Blazor supports event bubbling, where events propagate up the component hierarchy. You can prevent event propagation using the preventDefault method:

```
C#
```

```
<div @onclick="HandleOuterClick">

    <button @onclick="HandleInnerClick"
@onmousedown:preventDefault>Click me</button>

</div>


@code {

    private void HandleOuterClick()
```

```csharp
    {

        Console.WriteLine("Outer click");

    }


    private void HandleInnerClick()

    {

        Console.WriteLine("Inner click");

    }

}
```

In this example, clicking the button will only trigger HandleInnerClick because the preventDefault method prevents the event from bubbling up to the outer div.

Keyboard Events

Blazor supports keyboard events like onkeydown, onkeyup, and onkeypress:

```csharp
C#
<input type="text" @onkeydown="HandleKeyDown" />
```

```
@code {

    private void HandleKeyDown(KeyboardEventArgs
args)

    {

        if (args.Key == "Enter")

        {

            // Handle Enter key press

        }

    }

}
```

Best Practices

- Use clear and descriptive event handler names.
- Handle events efficiently to avoid performance issues.
- Consider using event delegation for better performance in some cases.
- Test your event handlers thoroughly.

By mastering event handling, you can create highly interactive and user-friendly Blazor applications.

Would you like to explore advanced event handling techniques or learn about specific event types?

Handling Events Effectively: Buttons, Forms, and More

Handling Events Effectively: Buttons, Forms, and More

Blazor provides a robust and efficient way to handle user interactions through events. Let's delve into how to effectively manage events for buttons, forms, and other UI elements.

Button Click Events

The most common interaction is a button click. You can handle this using the @onclick attribute:

```C#
<button class="btn btn-primary" @onclick="IncrementCount">Click me</button>

@code {

    private int count = 0;


    private void IncrementCount()
```

```
{
    count++;



    }

}
```

This code creates a button that increments a counter when clicked.

Form Submission

Blazor simplifies form handling with the `EditForm` component:

```C#
```

```
<EditForm Model="@person"
OnValidSubmit="HandleSubmit">

    <InputText @bind-Value="person.Name" />

    <InputText @bind-Value="person.Email" />

    <button type="submit">Submit</button>

</EditForm>


@code {

    public Person Person { get; set; } = new Person();


    private void HandleSubmit()

    {

        // Handle form submission

    }
```

```
public class Person

{

    public string Name { get; set; }

    public string Email { get; set; }

}

;
```

The **OnValidSubmit** event handler is invoked when the form is valid and submitted.

Input Change Events

To handle changes in input fields, use the **@onchange** or **@oninput** event:

```
C#
```

```
<input type="text" @bind-value="SearchTerm"
@oninput="HandleInputChange" />


@code {

    private string searchTerm = "";


    private void HandleInputChange(ChangeEventArgs
args)

    {

      searchTerm = args.Value.ToString();

      // Perform search

    }

  }
```

The `@oninput` event fires continuously as the user types, while `@onchange` fires when the input loses focus.

Keyboard Events

You can capture keyboard events using `@onkeydown`, `@onkeyup`, and `@onkeypress`:

```csharp
C#

<input type="text" @onkeydown="HandleKeyDown" />

@code {

    private void HandleKeyDown(KeyboardEventArgs args)

    {

        if (args.Key == "Enter")

        {
```

```
        // Handle Enter key press

    }

  }

}
```

Custom Events

For more complex scenarios, you can create custom events:

```C#
<CustomButton OnClick="HandleButtonClick" />


@code {

    private void HandleButtonClick()

    {
```

```csharp
// Handle button click

    }

}
```

```
C#
```

```razor
// CustomButton.razor

<button @onclick="() => OnClick?.Invoke()">Click
me</button>


[Parameter]

public EventCallback<MouseEventArgs> OnClick { get;
set; }
```

The CustomButton component raises a custom OnClick
event, which can be handled by the parent component.

Event Propagation

Blazor supports event bubbling, where events propagate up the component hierarchy. You can prevent this using preventDefault

```C#
<div @onclick="HandleOuterClick">

    <button @onclick="HandleInnerClick"
@onmousedown:preventDefault>Click me</button>

</div>
```

Clicking the inner button will only trigger HandleInnerClick

Best Practices

- Use clear and descriptive event handler names.

- Handle events efficiently to avoid performance issues.
- Consider using event delegation for better performance in some cases.
- Test your event handlers thoroughly.

By effectively handling events, you can create interactive and user-friendly Blazor applications.

Would you like to delve deeper into a specific aspect of event handling, such as advanced event arguments or custom event scenarios?

Understanding Cascading Parameters and Event Bubbling in Blazor

Understanding Cascading Parameters and Event Bubbling in Blazor

Cascading Parameters

Cascading parameters allow you to pass data down through a component hierarchy in Blazor. This is useful for sharing data between parent and child components without explicitly passing it through every intermediate component.

Example:

```C#
// ParentComponent.razor

<ChildComponent Value="42" />



// ChildComponent.razor

<p>Received value: @Value</p>



@code {

    [Parameter]
```

```csharp
public int Value { get; set; }

}
```

In this example, the Value property is cascaded from the
ParentComponent to the ChildComponent

Event Bubbling

Event bubbling is a mechanism where events propagate
up the component hierarchy. When an event occurs in a
child component, it can be handled by parent
components as well.

Example:

```csharp
C#
```

```
<div @onclick="HandleOuterClick">

    <button @onclick="HandleInnerClick">Click
me</button>
```

```
</div>


@code {

    private void HandleOuterClick()

    {

        Console.WriteLine("Outer click");

    }


    private void HandleInnerClick()

    {

        Console.WriteLine("Inner click");

    }

}
```

In this example, clicking the button will trigger both
`HandleInnerClick` and `HandleOuterClick`

Combining Cascading Parameters and Event Bubbling

You can combine cascading parameters and event bubbling to create complex component interactions. For instance, a child component can modify a value passed down from a parent component and then raise an event to notify the parent of the change.

Example:

```csharp
// ParentComponent.razor

<ChildComponent Value="@count"
OnValueChanged="@HandleValueChanged" />


<p>Parent count: @count</p>
```

```csharp
@code {

    private int count = 0;

    private void HandleValueChanged(int newValue)

    {

        count = newValue;

    }

}
```

C#

```razor
// ChildComponent.razor

<button @onclick="Increment">Increment</button>
```

```razor
<p>Child value: @Value</p>

@code {
    [Parameter]
    public int Value { get; set; }


    [Parameter]
    public EventCallback<int> OnValueChanged { get; set; }


    private void Increment()
    {
        Value++;
        OnValueChanged.InvokeAsync(Value);
```

```
        }

    }
```

In this example, the `ChildComponent` receives the `count` value from the parent as a cascading parameter. When the increment button is clicked, the `ChildComponent` increments its `Value` property and raises the `OnValueChanged` event, passing the new value back to the parent.

Best Practices

- Use cascading parameters judiciously to avoid overly complex component hierarchies.
- Consider using state management solutions for more complex data sharing scenarios.
- Handle events efficiently to prevent performance issues.
- Test your components thoroughly to ensure correct behavior.

By understanding cascading parameters and event bubbling, you can create more flexible and interactive Blazor components.

Would you like to explore advanced techniques for using cascading parameters and event bubbling, or perhaps delve into other aspects of component interaction?

Chapter 5

Styling Your Blazor Applications with CSS

Styling Your Blazor Applications with CSS

Blazor offers several ways to style your components, ensuring that your application has a consistent and visually appealing look.

Scoped CSS

This is the default approach in Blazor. CSS styles defined within a component are scoped to that component, preventing style conflicts.

```
C#
```

// Counter.razor

```razor
<p class="my-count">Current count: @currentCount</p>

@code {

    private int currentCount = 0;

}
```

Create a corresponding Counter.razor.css file:

```css
.my-count {

    color: blue;

    font-weight: bold;

}
```

Global CSS

For styles that apply to the entire application, create a `wwwroot/css/site.css` file and include global styles there.

```css
/* site.css */

body {

    font-family: Arial, sans-serif;

}
```

Inline Styles

For specific styling needs, you can use inline styles:

```csharp
<p style="color: red;">This text is red</p>
```

CSS Classes

You can apply CSS classes dynamically based on conditions:

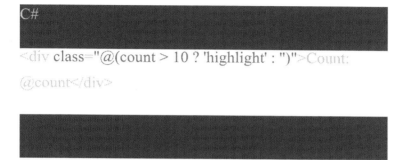

```
C#
<div class="@(count > 10 ? 'highlight' : "")">Count:
@count</div>
```

CSS Frameworks

Integrate popular CSS frameworks like Bootstrap or Tailwind CSS to accelerate development and improve UI consistency.

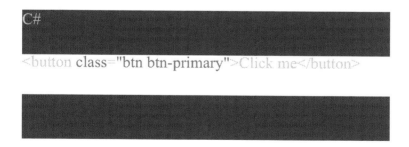

```
C#
<button class="btn btn-primary">Click me</button>
```

CSS Isolation

Blazor's CSS isolation prevents style conflicts between components. However, there are scenarios where you might need to override styles or apply global styles. You can use the `:host` selector to target the component itself or the `::deep` selector to target nested elements (use with caution).

```CSS
::deep .inner-element {

  color: green;

}
```

Best Practices

- Use a consistent styling approach throughout your application.
- Prefer scoped CSS for component-specific styles.

- Use global CSS for site-wide styles.
- Consider using CSS preprocessors like Sass or Less for better organization.
- Optimize CSS for performance by minimizing file size.
- Test your styles across different browsers and devices.

By effectively combining these techniques, you can create visually appealing and responsive Blazor applications.

Would you like to delve deeper into a specific aspect of styling, such as CSS preprocessors, styling components with complex layouts, or optimizing CSS performance?

Component-Level and Global Styling Options

Component-Level and Global Styling Options

Blazor offers flexible ways to style your components, ensuring both specificity and reusability.

Component-Level Styling

For styles that apply only to a specific component, use scoped CSS. This approach prevents style conflicts with other components:

```csharp
C#
```

```
// Counter.razor

<p class="my-count">Current count: @currentCount</p>


@code {

    private int currentCount = 0;

}
```

Create a corresponding Counter.razor.css file:

CSS

```css
.my-count {

    color: blue;

    font-weight: bold;

}
```

Styles defined in .razor.css files are automatically scoped to the component, preventing conflicts.

Global Styling

For styles that apply to the entire application, create a wwwroot/css/site.css file:

CSS

```css
/* site.css */
```

```
body {

    font-family: Arial, sans-serif;

}
```

Styles in `site.css` are global and can be overridden by component-level styles.

Inline Styles

For specific styling needs, use inline styles:

```C#
<p style="color: red;">This text is red</p>
```

However, avoid excessive use of inline styles as they can reduce maintainability.

CSS Classes

Dynamically apply CSS classes based on conditions:

```C#
```

```
<div class="@(count > 10 ? 'highlight' : '')">Count:
@count</div>
```

CSS Isolation

Blazor's CSS isolation ensures that styles are scoped to the component, preventing conflicts. However, you might need to override styles or apply global styles. Use the `:host` selector to target the component itself:

```CSS
:host {

    border: 1px solid black;

}
```

Best Practices

- Use scoped CSS for component-specific styles.
- Use global CSS for site-wide styles.
- Minimize inline styles.
- Consider using CSS preprocessors for better organization.
- Test your styles across different browsers and devices.

Additional Considerations

- **CSS Frameworks:** Integrate popular frameworks like Bootstrap or Tailwind CSS for rapid development.
- **CSS Preprocessors:** Use Sass or Less for variables, nesting, and other features.
- **Performance Optimization:** Minify and combine CSS files for better performance.

117

By effectively combining these techniques, you can create visually appealing and maintainable Blazor applications.

Would you like to explore advanced styling techniques, such as using CSS Grid or Flexbox for layout, or creating custom CSS themes?

Applying Bootstrap or Other CSS Frameworks

Applying Bootstrap or Other CSS Frameworks

CSS frameworks like Bootstrap provide pre-built CSS classes and components, accelerating development and ensuring consistent styling. Let's explore how to integrate Bootstrap into your Blazor application.

Including Bootstrap in Your Project

1. **Download Bootstrap**: Obtain the latest Bootstrap CSS and JavaScript files from the official website (https://getbootstrap.com/).
2. **Reference in** index.html: Include the Bootstrap CSS file in your wwwroot/index.html file within the <head> section:

HTML

```
<link rel="stylesheet"
href="~/lib/bootstrap/dist/css/bootstrap.min.css" />
```

Using Bootstrap Components

Bootstrap offers a vast array of pre-styled components, from buttons and navigation bars to forms and grids. Simply apply the appropriate CSS classes to your HTML elements:

C#

```html
<button type="button" class="btn btn-primary">Click me</button>

<div class="container">

  <div class="row">

    <div class="col-md-4">Column 1</div>

    <div class="col-md-4">Column 2</div>

    <div class="col-md-4">Column 3</div>




  </div>

</div>
```

Customizing Bootstrap

Bootstrap allows for customization through CSS overrides. Create a custom CSS file to modify existing styles or add new ones:

```css
CSS

/* custom.css */

.btn-primary {

    background-color: #007bff;

    border-color: #007bff;

}
```

Other CSS Frameworks

Besides Bootstrap, consider frameworks like Tailwind CSS, Foundation, or Bulma based on your project's

121

needs. Each framework has its own approach to styling and component structure.

Best Practices

- **Understand Bootstrap's structure**: Familiarize yourself with the grid system, components, and utility classes.
- **Customize selectively**: Only override necessary styles to maintain consistency.
- **Consider responsiveness**: Ensure your application looks good on different screen sizes.
- **Performance optimization**: Minimize the number of Bootstrap components and CSS files to improve load times.
- **Combine with custom CSS**: Use custom CSS for unique styling requirements.

Example: Creating a Basic Layout

```C#
```

122

```html
<div class="container">
  <div class="row">
    <div class="col-md-4">
      <h2>Sidebar</h2>
      <ul class="list-group">
        <li class="list-group-item">Item 1</li>
        <li class="list-group-item">Item 2</li>
      </ul>
    </div>
    <div class="col-md-8">
      <h2>Main Content</h2>
      <p>This is the main content area.</p>
    </div>
  </div>
</div>
```

```
</div>
```

This code creates a basic layout using Bootstrap's grid system, with a sidebar and main content area.

By effectively utilizing CSS frameworks, you can significantly accelerate your development process and create visually appealing and responsive web applications.

Would you like to explore specific CSS frameworks in more detail or discuss advanced styling techniques?

Chapter 6

Working with Data in Blazor WebAssembly

Working with Data in Blazor WebAssembly

Blazor WebAssembly provides powerful tools for fetching, displaying, and managing data. Let's explore how to effectively work with data in your Blazor applications.

Fetching Data

To fetch data from an API, use HttpClient:

```C#

@inject HttpClient Http
```

```
<ul>
```

```razor
@foreach (var weatherForecast in forecasts)

    {

        <li>@weatherForecast.Date.ToShortDateString():
@weatherForecast.Summary</li>

    }

</ul>


@code {

    private WeatherForecast[] forecasts;


    protected override async Task OnInitializedAsync()

    {

        forecasts = await
Http.GetFromJsonAsync<WeatherForecast[]>("sample-d
ata/weather.json");
```

```
public class WeatherForecast
{
    public DateTime Date { get; set; }

    public int TemperatureC { get; set; }

    public string? Summary { get; set;
```

```
}

  }

}

```

Displaying Data

Use `@foreach` to iterate over collections and display data:

```csharp
<ul>

  @foreach (var item in items)

  {

    <li>@item</li>
```

```
        }
</ul>
```

Data Binding

Bind data to UI elements for two-way synchronization:

```csharp
<input type="text" @bind-value="Name" />
<p>Hello, @Name!</p>

@code {
    public string Name { get; set; }
}
```

```
```

Handling Data Changes

Use `NotifyPropertyChanged` or state management
solutions to update the UI when data changes:

```csharp

[NotifyPropertyChanged]

public class Person

{

    public string Name { get; set; }

}
```

Data Validation

Validate user input using data annotations or custom
validation logic:

```csharp
<EditForm Model="@person"
OnValidSubmit="HandleSubmit">

    <InputText @bind-Value="person.Name" />

    <DataAnnotationsValidator />

    <ValidationSummary />

    <button type="submit">Submit</button>

</EditForm>


@code {

    public Person Person { get; set; } = new Person();
```

```
private void HandleSubmit()
{
    // Handle form submission
}


public class Person
{
    [Required]
    public string Name { get; set; }
}
```

Best Practices

* Use `HttpClient` for fetching data.

* Prefer JSON for data serialization.

* Handle errors gracefully.

* Optimize data fetching and rendering.

* Consider using state management solutions for complex data scenarios.

* Validate user input to ensure data integrity.

By following these guidelines, you can effectively manage data in your Blazor applications.

Would you like to delve deeper into a specific aspect of data handling, such as state management, data validation, or performance optimization?

Handling API Responses and Displaying Data

Handling API Responses and Displaying Data

Blazor excels at fetching and displaying data from APIs. Let's explore how to effectively handle API responses and present the data to users.

Fetching Data with HttpClient

Blazor's HttpClient simplifies the process of making HTTP requests:

```C#
@inject HttpClient Http
```

```
<ul>

    @foreach (var todo in todos)

    {

        <li>@todo.Title</li>

    }

</ul>


@code {

    private Todo[] todos = Array.Empty<Todo>();


    protected override async Task OnInitializedAsync()

    {

        todos = await
Http.GetFromJsonAsync<Todo[]>("todos");
```

```csharp
    }

public class Todo
{
    public int Id { get; set; }

    public string Title { get; set; } = string.Empty;

    public bool Completed { get; set; }
}

}
```

Error Handling

Implement error handling to gracefully handle API failures:

```csharp
C#
```

```csharp
protected override async Task OnInitializedAsync()
{
    try
    {
        todos = await Http.GetFromJsonAsync<Todo[]>("todos");
    }
    catch (Exception ex)
    {
        Console.Error.WriteLine($"Error fetching data: {ex}");
        // Handle error, e.g., display an error message
    }
}
```

Displaying Data

Use @foreach to iterate over collections and display data:

```csharp
<ul>

    @foreach (var todo in todos)

    {

        <li>@todo.Title</li>

    }

</ul>
```

Data Binding

Bind properties to UI elements for dynamic updates:

```csharp
```

```
<input type="text" @bind-value="selectedTodo.Title" />
```

```
@code {

    private Todo selectedTodo;

}
```

Data Formatting

Format data for display using string interpolation or
formatting methods:

```C#
<p>Total: @{todos.Sum(t => t.Price)}</p>
```

Loading States

Indicate loading state to the user:

```C#
@if (forecasts == null)
{
    <p>Loading...</p>
}
else
{
    // Display data
}
```

Pagination

Handle large datasets efficiently using pagination:

```csharp
<button @onclick="PreviousPage">Previous</button>

<button @onclick="NextPage">Next</button>


@code {

    private int pageIndex = 0;

    private int pageSize = 10;

    private Todo[] todos = Array.Empty<Todo>();



    // ...

}
```

Best Practices

- Use asynchronous programming for API calls.
- Handle errors gracefully.
- Optimize data fetching and rendering.
- Consider using state management for complex data scenarios.
- Implement loading indicators.
- Test your data handling code thoroughly.

By following these guidelines, you can effectively fetch, handle, and display data in your Blazor applications.

Would you like to delve deeper into a specific aspect of data handling, such as data validation, state management, or optimizing performance?

Introduction to Dependency Injection for Data Services in Blazor WebAssembly

Introduction to Dependency Injection for Data Services in Blazor WebAssembly

142

Dependency Injection (DI) is a powerful technique for managing dependencies in your application. In Blazor, it's crucial for handling data services efficiently.

Understanding Dependency Injection

DI is a software design pattern where objects get dependencies from external sources rather than creating them themselves. This promotes loose coupling, testability, and maintainability.

Setting Up Dependency Injection in Blazor

Blazor provides built-in support for DI. To register a service:

```C#
builder.Services.AddScoped<IWeatherForecastService, WeatherForecastService>();
```

- **AddScoped** creates a new instance of the service for each request. Other options include **AddTransient** and **AddSingleton**
- **IWeatherForecastService** is the interface defining the service.
- **WeatherForecastService** is the implementation.

Consuming Services in Components

Inject the service into your component using constructor injection:

```
C#

@inject IWeatherForecastService ForecastService


protected override async Task UnInitialized Async()
{
    Forecasts = await
ForecastService.GetForecastAsync();
```

Creating a Data Service

Define an interface for your data service:

```C#
public interface IWeatherForecastService
{

    Task<WeatherForecast[]> GetForecastAsync();

}
```

Implement the service:

```C#
public class WeatherForecastService :
IWeatherForecastService
```

145

```csharp
{
    private readonly HttpClient _http;

    public WeatherForecastService(HttpClient http)
    {
        _http = http;
    }

    public async Task<WeatherForecast[]>
GetForecastAsync()
```

```
    {
        return await
_http.GetFromJsonAsync<WeatherForecast[]>("sample-
data/weather.json");
    }
}
```

Benefits of Dependency Injection

- Loose coupling: Components depend on
  abstractions, not concrete implementations.

- **Testability:** Easily mock or stub dependencies for testing.
- **Maintainability:** Improves code organization and reduces dependencies between components.
- **Reusability:** Services can be reused in different parts of the application.

Best Practices

- Use interfaces to define service contracts.
- Register services in `Program.cs`
- Inject services into components using constructor injection.
- Consider using scoped or transient lifetimes for most services.
- Test your services thoroughly.

Additional Considerations

- **Lifetime management:** Choose the appropriate service lifetime based on your requirements.

148

- **Error handling:** Implement proper error handling in your data services.
- **Performance optimization:** Optimize data fetching and processing for large datasets.
- **Dependency injection frameworks:** Explore third-party DI frameworks for advanced scenarios.

By effectively using dependency injection, you can create well-structured, maintainable, and testable Blazor applications.

Would you like to delve deeper into a specific aspect of dependency injection, such as service lifetimes, testing, or advanced scenarios?

Chapter 7

State Management in Blazor Applications

State Management in Blazor Applications

Effective state management is crucial for building complex Blazor applications. Let's explore different approaches and their use cases.

Component State

Component state is managed within a component itself. It's suitable for local states that don't need to be shared across components.

```C#
@page "/counter"

<h3>Counter</h3>

<p>Current count: @currentCount</p>

<button class="btn btn-primary"
@onclick="IncrementCount">Click me</button>
```

```
@code {

private int currentCount



= 0;


private void IncrementCount()

{

currentCount++;




}
```

151

```
}
```

Service State

Use a service to manage shared state accessible across multiple components:

```csharp
public class CounterService

{

    public int Count { get; set; }

}
```

```
@inject CounterService CounterService
```

```
<p>Count: @CounterService.Count</p>
```

```
<button
@onclick="IncrementCount">Increment</button>


@code {

    private void IncrementCount()

    {

        CounterService.Count++;

    }

}
```

Application State

For global state shared across the entire application, consider using a state management library or a custom state store.

- Blazor State: Provides a flexible state management solution.
- Redux: A popular state management pattern adapted for Blazor.

Custom State Store:

```csharp
C#

public class AppState

{

    public int Counter { get; set; }

}
```

```
@inject AppState AppState
```

```
<p>Count: @AppState.Counter</p>
```

```
<button

@onclick="IncrementCount">Increment</button>


@code {

  private void IncrementCount()

  {

    AppState.Counter++;

  }

}
```

Persisted State

Store state outside the application for persistence across sessions:

- Local Storage

- Session Storage
- Cookies

```csharp
C#

@inject ILocalStorage LocalStorage


protected override async Task UnInitialized Async()

{

    var countString = await
LocalStorage.GetItemAsync<string>("count");

    if (int.TryParse(countString, out var count))

    {

        CurrentCount = count;

    }

}
```

```
private async Task SaveCount()

{

    await LocalStorage.SetItemAsync("count",
CurrentCount.ToString());

}
```

Choosing the Right Approach

- **Component state:** For local state within a component.
- **Service state:** For shared state across multiple components.
- **Application state:** For global state accessible throughout the app.
- **Persisted state:** For state that needs to persist across sessions.

Best Practices

- Use component state for simple scenarios.
- Employ service state for shared data that doesn't require global access.
- Choose a suitable state management library for complex applications.
- Consider performance implications when using persisted state.
- Test your state management implementation thoroughly.

By understanding these state management techniques, you can effectively manage data flow in your Blazor applications.

Would you like to delve deeper into a specific state management approach or explore advanced techniques?

Implementing Application State with Blazor State Management Library

Implementing Application State with Blazor State Management Library

Blazor State Management (BSM) is a popular library for managing application state in Blazor applications. It provides a structured approach to handling complex state scenarios.

Setting up Blazor State Management

1. Install the Blazor State Management NuGet package:

2. Bash

```
dotnet add package BlazorState
```

3.

5. Register the Blaze State Extension in Program.cs

6. C#

builder.Services.AddBlazorState();

7.

Creating a State Store

Define a state store to hold application-wide data:

```C#

public class CounterState : State<CounterState>
{
    public int Count { get; set; }

    public void Increment()
    {
        Count++;
    }
}
```

Accessing State in Components

Inject the `IState<CounterState>` interface into your component:

```C#
@inject IState<CounterState> CounterState

<p>Count: @CounterState.Value.Count</p>
<button
@onclick="IncrementCount">Increment</button>

@code {
    private void IncrementCount()
    {
        CounterState.Value.Increment();
    }
}
```

Dispatching Actions

Blazor State supports actions for triggering state updates:

```csharp
C#
public class IncrementCounterAction : IAction
{

}


@inject IState<CounterState> CounterState
@inject IDispatcher Dispatcher

<button
@onclick="IncrementCount">Increment</button>

@code {
    private void IncrementCount()
    {
```

```
        Dispatcher.Dispatch(new
IncrementCounterAction());
    }
}
```

The **IncrementCounterAction** doesn't contain any data, but it can if needed.

Handling Actions in the State

Implement a reducer to handle actions and update state:

```C#
public class CounterState : State<CounterState>
{
    public override void Initialize()
    {
        // Initial state
    }
```

163

```
public void Reduce(IncrementCounterAction action)
{

    Count++;

}
}
```

Additional Features

- **Selectors:** Create derived state from the main state.
- **Effects:** Perform side effects like API calls after state updates.
- **Middleware:** Intercept and modify actions or state updates.

Best Practices

- Use clear and descriptive state names.
- Break down complex state into smaller states.
- Consider using selectors for derived data.

- Handle errors gracefully.
- Test your state management implementation.

Comparison to Other Approaches

Blazor State Management offers a structured approach with features like selectors, effects, and middleware compared to manual state management or service-based approaches.

By using Blazor State Management, you can effectively manage complex state in your Blazor applications, improving code organization, testability, and maintainability.

Would you like to explore advanced features of Blazor State Management, such as selectors, effects, and middleware?

Sharing State Between Components Effectively

Sharing State Between Components Effectively

In Blazor, effectively sharing state between components is crucial for building complex applications. Let's explore several techniques to achieve this.

Lifting State Up

This involves moving the shared state to a common ancestor component. Child components can then access and modify the state through properties:

```C#
// ParentComponent.razor
<p>Shared count: @count</p>
<ChildComponent Count="@count"
OnCountChanged="@HandleCountChanged" />
```

```csharp
@code {
    private int count = 0;

    private void HandleCountChanged(int newCount)
    {
        count = newCount;
    }
}


// ChildComponent.razor
<button
@onclick="IncrementCount">Increment</button>

@code {
    [Parameter] public int Count { get; set; }
    [Parameter] public EventCallback<int>
OnCountChanged { get; set; }

    private void IncrementCount()
    {
        OnCountChanged.InvokeAsync(Count + 1);
    }
```

}

Using a Shared Service

For more complex scenarios, create a shared service to manage state:

```
C#
public class CounterService
{
    public int Count { get; set; }
}

@inject CounterService CounterService

<p>Count: @CounterService.Count</p>
<button
@onclick="IncrementCount">Increment</button>

@code {
```

```csharp
private void IncrementCount()
{
    CounterService.Count++;
}
}
```

Leveraging State Management Libraries

For large-scale applications, consider using a state management library like Blazor State:

```csharp
public class CounterState : State<CounterState>
{
    public int Count { get; set; }

    public void Increment()
    {
        Count++;
    }
```

169

```razor
}

@inject IState<CounterState> CounterState

<p>Count: @CounterState.Value.Count</p>
<button
@onclick="IncrementCount">Increment</button>

@code {
    private void IncrementCount()
    {
        CounterState.Value.Increment();
    }
}
```

Context API (Similar to React Context)

While not a built-in feature, you can implement a custom Context API:

```csharp
C#

public class CountContext : ComponentBase
{
    public int Count { get; set; }

    public static readonly new Func<CountContext>
    Default = () => new CountContext();
}

<CountContext.Provider Value="42">
    <ChildComponent />
</CountContext.Provider>
```

Choosing the Right Approach

- **Lifting state up:** Suitable for simple state sharing between closely related components.
- **Shared service:** Ideal for global state or complex state management.

- **State management libraries:** Recommended for large-scale applications with complex state requirements.
- **Custom Context API:** Can be used for specific scenarios, but requires more implementation effort.

Best Practices

- Consider the scope of the state when choosing a method.
- Avoid excessive prop drilling by lifting state up or using a shared service.
- Use state management libraries for complex applications with multiple interrelated components.
- Optimize state updates to prevent performance issues.

By effectively sharing state between components, you can build more maintainable and scalable Blazor applications.

Would you like to delve deeper into a specific state management technique or explore advanced use cases?

Chapter 8

Persisting Data in Blazor WebAssembly

Persisting Data in Blazor WebAssembly

Blazor WebAssembly, being a client-side framework, requires specific strategies for persisting data. Here are some common approaches:

Local Storage

Local storage persists data within the user's browser for the lifetime of the application.

```
C#
```

```
@inject ILocalStorage LocalStorage

protected override async Task UnInitialized Async()
{
    var countString = await
LocalStorage.GetItemAsync<string>("count");
    if (int.TryParse(countString, out var count))
    {
        CurrentCount = count;
    }
}

private async Task SaveCount()
{
    await LocalStorage.SetItemAsync("count",
CurrentCount.ToString());
}
```

Session Storage

Similar to local storage but data is cleared when the browser session ends:

```C#
@inject ISessionStorage SessionStorage
```

// ... similar usage as LocalStorage

IndexedDB

For more complex data structures and larger amounts of data, IndexedDB is a suitable option:

```C#
@inject IDbFactory DbFactory
```

private IDatabase db;

protected override async Task UnInitialized Async()
{

```
db = await DbFactory.OpenAsync("myDatabase", 1);
// ... create object stores
}
```

Server-Side Storage

For sensitive or large datasets, consider persisting data on the server using:

- **HTTP APIs:** Send data to a server-side API for storage.
- **SignalR:** Real-time communication for data synchronization.
- **Blazor Server:** For full-stack development, leverage server-side storage.

Best Practices

- **Security: Avoid storing** sensitive data in client-side storage.

176

- **Data Format:** Choose appropriate data formats (JSON, binary) based on data size and complexity.
- **Performance:** Optimize data access and storage operations for performance.
- **Error Handling:** Implement proper error handling for storage operations.
- **Data Synchronization:** Consider data synchronization mechanisms for server-side storage.

Considerations

- **Data Size:** For large datasets, consider server-side storage or IndexedDB.
- **Data Sensitivity:** Avoid storing sensitive data in client-side storage.
- **Data Lifetime:** Choose between local storage, session storage, or server-side storage based on data lifetime requirements.

- **Performance:** Optimize data access and storage operations for performance.
- **User Experience:** Provide feedback to the user during data saving operations.

By carefully considering these factors and choosing the appropriate persistence mechanism, you can effectively manage data in your Blazor WebAssembly applications.

Would you like to delve deeper into a specific persistence method or explore data synchronization techniques?

Integrating Blazor with IndexedDB for Persistent Storage

Integrating Blazor with IndexedDB for Persistent Storage

IndexedDB is a powerful browser API for storing structured data. Let's explore how to integrate it with Blazor for persistent storage.

Understanding IndexedDB

IndexedDB is a NoSQL database that allows storing large amounts of structured data. It's asynchronous, providing better performance and user experience.

Setting Up IndexedDB in Blazor

```C#
@inject IDbFactory DbFactory

private IDatabase db;

protected override async Task OnInitializedAsync()
{
    db = await DbFactory.OpenAsync("myDatabase", 1);
    var objectStore = db.CreateObjectStore("todos");
```

}

Creating an Object Store

Object stores are containers for data.

```C#
var objectStore = db.CreateObjectStore("todos", new
ObjectStoreParameters
{
    KeyPath = "id",
    AutoIncrement = true
});
```

This creates an object store named "todos" with an
auto-incrementing key path "id".

Storing Data

```csharp
private async Task AddTodo(Todo todo)
{
    var transaction = db.CreateTransaction("todos", "readwrite");
    var objectStore = transaction.GetObjectStore("todos");
    await objectStore.AddAsync(todo);
    await transaction.Completed;
}
```

Retrieving Data

```csharp
private async Task<Todo[]> GetTodos()
{
    var transaction = db.CreateTransaction("todos");
    var objectStore = transaction.GetObjectStore("todos");
    var cursor = await objectStore.OpenCursorAsync();
```

```csharp
var todos = new List<Todo>();
while (cursor.Valid)
{
    todos.Add((Todo)cursor.Value);
    await cursor.ContinueAsync();
}

return todos.ToArray();
}
```

Updating Data

```csharp
C#
private async Task UpdateTodo(Todo todo)
{
    var transaction = db.CreateTransaction("todos",
"readwrite");
    var objectStore = transaction.GetObjectStore("todos");
    await objectStore.PutAsync(todo, todo.id);
```

```
await transaction.Completed;
}
```

Deleting Data

```csharp
C#

private async Task DeleteTodo(int id)
{
    var transaction = db.CreateTransaction("todos",
"readwrite");
    var objectStore = transaction.GetObjectStore("todos");
    await objectStore.DeleteAsync(id);
    await transaction.Completed;
}
```

Handling Errors

Always handle errors using try-catch blocks:

183

```csharp
C#

try
{
    // IndexedDB operations
}
catch (Exception ex)
{
    // Handle error
}
```

Best Practices

- Use meaningful object store names.
- Create indexes for efficient querying.
- Handle errors gracefully.
- Consider using transactions for atomic operations.
- Optimize data structures for performance.
- Test your IndexedDB implementation thoroughly.

Considerations

- **Browser compatibility**: IndexedDB support varies across browsers.
- Asynchronous operations: Handle asynchronous nature effectively.
- Data complexity: IndexedDB is suitable for complex data structures.
- Performance: Optimize queries and data access for performance.

Additional Tips

- Use a wrapper class to simplify IndexedDB interactions.
- Consider using a third-party library for added features.
- Explore IndexedDB's advanced features like key paths and indexes.

By effectively utilizing IndexedDB, you can store and manage significant amounts of data within your Blazor WebAssembly applications.

Would you like to delve deeper into a specific aspect of IndexedDB or explore alternative storage options?

Part I:

Blazor WebAssembly Fundamentals

Blazor WebAssembly Fundamentals

Blazor WebAssembly is a framework for building interactive web UIs using C# instead of JavaScript. It runs client-side in the browser, offering a full-stack development experience with the .NET ecosystem.

Core Concepts

- **Components:** Reusable building blocks of Blazor applications, combining HTML, CSS, and C# code.
- **Razor Syntax:** A syntax for embedding C# code within HTML templates.
- **Data Binding:** Seamlessly connecting C# properties to UI elements for automatic updates.
- **Lifecycle Methods:** Methods invoked at different stages of a component's lifecycle.
- **Routing:** Navigating between different pages or views in a Blazor app.

Creating a Basic Blazor App

To start, create a new Blazor WebAssembly project using the .NET CLI:

```bash
Bash

dotnet new blazorwasm -o MyBlazorApp
```

Replace MyBlazorApp with your desired project name.

Building Your First Component

Replace the contents of Pages/Index.razor with:

```C#
<h1>Hello, world!</h1>


<button class="btn btn-primary"
@onclick="IncrementCount">Click me</button>
<p>You clicked @currentCount times</p>


@code {
    private int currentCount = 0;


    private void IncrementCount()
    {
```

```
    currentCount++;

    }

}
```

This creates a simple counter component.

Data Binding

Blazor supports two-way data binding:

```csharp
<input type="text" @bind-value="Name" />

<p>Hello, @Name!</p>


@code {

    public string Name { get; set; }

}
```

Routing

Navigate between pages using the Router component:

```csharp
C#
```

```
<Router
AppAssembly="@typeof(Program).Assembly">
    <Route Path="/" Component="{typeof(Index)}" />
    <Route Path="/counter"
Component="{typeof(Counter)}" />
    <Route Path="/fetchdata"
Component="{typeof(FetchData)}" />
</Router>
```

Dependency Injection

Blazor supports dependency injection (DI) for managing
services:

```C#
@inject HttpClient Http


protected override async Task OnInitializedAsync()
{
    WeatherForecast[] forecasts = await
Http.GetFromJsonAsync<WeatherForecast[]>("sample-d
ata/weather.json");
}
```

Lifecycle Methods

Methods like OnInitialized, OnParametersSet, and
OnAfterRender are called at different stages of a
component's lifecycle.

Additional Tips

- **Leverage C# features:** Use LINQ, async/await, and other C# constructs.
- **Create reusable components:** Modularize your UI.
- **Handle errors gracefully:** Implement error handling mechanisms.
- **Optimize performance:** Consider performance implications when building complex UIs.
- **Explore state management:** Use libraries like Blazor State for complex state scenarios.

By understanding these fundamentals, you can build robust Blazor WebAssembly applications.

Would you like to delve deeper into a specific area, such as component lifecycle, data binding, or routing?

Chapter 9:

Optimizing and Deploying Blazor WebAssembly Apps

Optimizing and Deploying Blazor WebAssembly Apps

Optimizing Blazor WebAssembly Apps

Optimizing your Blazor WebAssembly app is crucial for delivering a fast and responsive user experience.

Performance Tips:

- Minimize JavaScript interop: Use it sparingly as it can impact performance.
- Optimize component rendering: Use `ShouldRender` to control component re-renders.
- Leverage lazy loading: Load components only when needed.
- Optimize image and asset loading: Use appropriate formats and compression.

```csharp
C#

protected override bool ShouldRender()
{
    // Perform logic to determine if component should re-render
    return base.ShouldRender();
}
```

Deploying Blazor WebAssembly Apps

194

Static File Hosting:

- **Azure Static Web Apps:** Offers built-in support for Blazor WebAssembly.
- **AWS S3:** Configure S3 bucket to host static files.
- **Netlify:** Provides platform for deploying static sites.
- **GitHub Pages:** Host your app directly from GitHub repository.

Containerization:

- **Docker:** Create a Docker image and deploy to platforms like Azure Container Instances, AWS ECS, or Kubernetes.

Serverless Functions:

- **Azure Functions:** Use Azure Functions to serve Blazor WebAssembly app as a static website.
- **AWS Lambda:** Similar to Azure Functions, but on AWS.

Custom Hosting:

- **Configure web server:** Set up IIS, Apache, or Nginx to serve your Blazor app.

Code Example (Dockerfile):

```
Dockerfile

FROM mcr.microsoft.com/dotnet/aspnet:6.0 AS base
WORKDIR /app
COPY *.dll ./


FROM mcr.microsoft.com/dotnet/aspnet:6.0-alpine AS publish
WORKDIR /app
COPY --from=base /app *.dll ./


ENTRYPOINT ["dotnet", "YourApp.dll"]
```

Deployment Considerations

- **Performance optimization**: Optimize your app for the target environment.
- **Security**: Implement appropriate security measures.
- **Scalability**: Consider your application's scaling needs.
- **Cost**: Evaluate the cost implications of different deployment options.
- **Continuous integration and deployment (CI/CD)**: Automate the build and deployment process.

Additional Tips:

- **Progressive Web App (PWA)**: Consider converting your app into a PWA for offline capabilities.
- **Content Delivery Network (CDN)**: Use a CDN to improve performance and reduce latency.
- **Monitoring and logging**: Implement monitoring to track app performance and identify issues.

By following these guidelines, you can effectively optimize and deploy your Blazor WebAssembly applications.

Would you like to delve deeper into a specific deployment option or explore advanced optimization techniques?

Chapter 10:

Deployment Options for Blazor WebAssembly Applications

Deployment Options for Blazor WebAssembly Applications

Blazor WebAssembly applications can be deployed in various ways, each with its own advantages and considerations. Let's explore the primary options:

Static File Hosting

This is the most common approach for deploying Blazor WebAssembly apps. It involves hosting the compiled application's static files on a web server.

Platforms:

- **Azure Static Web Apps:** Offers built-in support for Blazor WebAssembly, including CI/CD, custom domains, and free tier options.
- **AWS S3:** Can be configured to host static websites, providing flexibility and scalability.
- **Netlify:** A platform-as-a-service (PaaS) specializing in static websites with features like serverless functions.
- **GitHub Pages:** Host your app directly from a GitHub repository, ideal for open-source projects.

Containerization

Deploying as a container offers flexibility and scalability.

Platforms:

- **Docker:** Create a Docker image containing your Blazor app and its dependencies.
- **Azure Container Instances:** Deploy Docker containers without managing infrastructure.

```
Dockerfile

FROM mcr.microsoft.com/dotnet/aspnet:6.0 AS base
WORKDIR /app
COPY *.dll ./

FROM mcr.microsoft.com/dotnet/aspnet:6.0-alpine AS publish
WORKDIR /app
COPY --from=base /app *.dll ./

ENTRYPOINT ["dotnet", "YourApp.dll"]
```

Serverless Functions

Serverless functions can host Blazor WebAssembly apps, providing scalability and cost-efficiency.

Platforms:

- **Azure Functions:** Create a function to serve the static assets of your Blazor app.
- **AWS Lambda:** Similar to Azure Functions, but on AWS.

Custom Hosting

For full control, configure a web server to host your Blazor app.

Servers:

- **IIS:** Microsoft's web server.
- **Apache:** Open-source web server.
- **Nginx:** High-performance web server.

Considerations

202

- **Performance:** Static file hosting often provides better performance due to direct asset delivery.
- **Scalability:** Containerization and serverless functions offer horizontal scaling.
- **Cost:** Evaluate pricing models for different platforms.
- **Security:** Implement appropriate security measures for each deployment option.
- **Deployment process:** Consider CI/CD pipelines for automated deployments.

Additional Tips

- **Optimize for the target platform:** Consider platform-specific optimizations.
- **Use a CDN:** Improve performance by distributing content across multiple servers.
- **Implement Progressive Web App (PWA) features:** Enhance user experience with offline capabilities.

- Monitor performance: Track application performance and identify bottlenecks.

By carefully considering these factors and choosing the appropriate deployment option, you can successfully deploy your Blazor WebAssembly applications.

Would you like to delve deeper into a specific deployment option or explore advanced deployment strategies?

Part II:

Advanced Topics

Chapter 11:

Beyond the Basics: Advanced Blazor Techniques

Beyond the Basics: Advanced Blazor Techniques

Blazor offers a robust foundation for building web applications, but to truly master it, you need to explore advanced techniques.

Component Lifecycle Management

Understanding the full component lifecycle is crucial for optimizing performance and managing complex state:

```csharp
C#

protected override void OnInitialized()
{
    // Perform initial setup
}

protected override void OnParametersSet()
{
    // Handle parameter changes
}
```

```csharp
protected override Task OnAfterRenderAsync(bool
firstRender)
{
    if (firstRender)
    {
        // Perform actions after first render
    }

    return base.OnAfterRenderAsync(firstRender);
}
```

JavaScript Interop

Access browser APIs or JavaScript libraries:

```csharp
C#
[JSInvokable]
public static async Task<string>
GetLocalStorageItem(string key)
{
```

```
return await
JSRuntime.InvokeAsync<string>("localStorage.getItem"
, key);
}
```

Custom Components

Create reusable components with custom logic and
parameters:

```C#
<MyCustomComponent Title="Hello, World!" />

@code {
    [Parameter]
    public string Title { get; set; }
}
```

Dependency Injection

Leverage DI for managing services and dependencies:

```C#
```

@inject IMyService MyService

protected override void OnInitialized()
{
    var data = await MyService.GetDataAsync();
}

State Management

For complex state management, consider using a state management library like Blazor State or Redux:

```C#
```

@inject IState<CounterState> CounterState

```
<p>Count: @CounterState.Value.Count</p>
<button
@onclick="IncrementCount">Increment</button>

@code {
    private void IncrementCount()
    {
        CounterState.Value.Increment();
    }
}
```

Performance Optimization

- Use ShouldRender to control component re-renders.
- Minimize JavaScript interop.
- Optimize component rendering.
- Leverage lazy loading.
- Profile your application to identify performance bottlenecks.

Advanced Routing

Explore route parameters, query strings, and navigation options:

```csharp
<Route Path="/products/{id:int}"
Component="{typeof(ProductDetails)}" />
```

Testing

Write unit and integration tests for your components:

```csharp
[Fact]
public void Counter_Increments_Count()
{
    // Arrange
    var counter = new Counter();
```

```
// Act
counter.IncrementCount();

// Assert
Assert.Equal(1, counter.currentCount);
}
```

Additional Techniques

- **WebAssembly Interop:** Directly call WebAssembly functions from C#.
- **Blazor Hybrid:** Combine Blazor WebAssembly with Blazor Server.
- **Server-Side Blazor:** Explore differences and similarities between the two models.

By mastering these advanced techniques, you can build more complex and efficient Blazor applications.

Would you like to delve deeper into a specific
advanced topic, such as performance optimization,
state management, or testing?

Chapter 12:

Authentication and
Authorization in Blazor

Authentication and Authorization in Blazor

Authentication and authorization are critical aspects of building secure web applications. Blazor provides mechanisms to implement these features effectively.

Authentication

Authentication is the process of verifying a user's identity. Blazor relies on external authentication providers like IdentityServer, OAuth, or OpenID Connect.

Key steps:

1. Configure authentication provider: Set up the authentication provider in your backend API.

2. **Implement authentication state provider:** Create a custom authentication state provider to manage user authentication state.

3. **Use AuthorizeView component:** Protect components based on user roles.

```csharp
C#

@inject AuthenticationStateProvider
AuthenticationStateProvider

protected override async Task OnInitializedAsync()
{
    var authState = await
AuthenticationStateProvider.GetAuthenticationStateAsync();
```

```
var user = authState.User;
if (user.Identity.IsAuthenticated)
{
    // User
```

is authenticated

```
    }
}
```

Authorization

Authorization determines what a user can do after authentication. Blazor uses policy-based authorization.

Key steps:

1. **Define policies:** Create authorization policies based on user roles or claims.

2. **Apply policies to components:** Use the 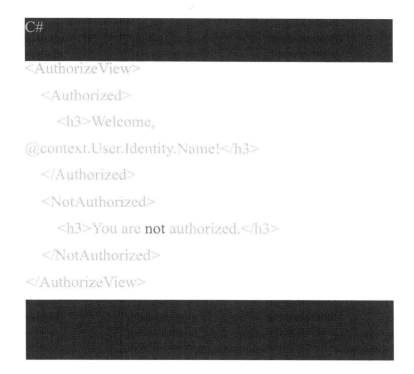AuthorizeView component with the Authorized and NotAuthorized templates.

```
C#
```

```
<AuthorizeView>
  <Authorized>
    <h3>Welcome,
@context.User.Identity.Name!</h3>
  </Authorized>
  <NotAuthorized>
    <h3>You are not authorized.</h3>
  </NotAuthorized>
</AuthorizeView>
```

Implementing a Custom Authentication State Provider

```
C#
```

```csharp
public class CustomAuthenticationStateProvider :
AuthenticationStateProvider
{
    private readonly HttpClient _httpClient;

    public CustomAuthenticationStateProvider(HttpClient

httpClient)
    {
        _httpClient = httpClient;
    }

    public override async Task<AuthenticationState>
```

```
GetAuthenticationStateAsync()
    {
    // Implement logic to retrieve user information from
the server or local storage
    var user = new ClaimsPrincipal(new
ClaimsIdentity(new[]
        {
        new Claim(ClaimTypes.Name, "John Doe"),
        new Claim(ClaimTypes.Role, "Admin")
        }, "Custom"));
    return new AuthenticationState(user);
    }
}
```

Best Practices

- Use strong password hashing and encryption.
- Protect sensitive data.

- Implement multi-factor authentication.
- Regularly update authentication libraries.
- Test authentication and authorization thoroughly.

Additional Considerations

- **Token-based authentication:** Use JWT or other token-based mechanisms for stateless authentication.
- **Role-based access control (RBAC):** Define roles and permissions based on user roles.
- **Claim-based authorization:** Use claims to make fine-grained authorization decisions.
- **Secure data transmission:** Protect sensitive data during transmission.
- **User experience:** Provide clear feedback to users about authentication and authorization status.

By following these guidelines and leveraging the built-in features of Blazor, you can implement robust authentication and authorization in your web applications.

Would you like to delve deeper into a specific authentication or authorization technique, or explore advanced scenarios like social login or single sign-on?

Chapter 13:

Debugging and
Troubleshooting Blazor
WebAssembly

Part III:

Community and Resources

Debugging and Troubleshooting Blazor WebAssembly

Effective debugging is essential for developing robust
Blazor WebAssembly applications. Let's explore
common issues and troubleshooting techniques.

Browser Developer Tools

The browser's developer tools are invaluable for debugging Blazor apps.

- **Console:** View errors, warnings, and log messages.
- **Network:** Inspect network requests and responses.
- **Elements:** Inspect the DOM structure and CSS styles.
- **Performance:** Analyze application performance.

Blazor-Specific Debugging

- **Blazor Profiler:** Use the built-in profiler to analyze component rendering and performance.
- **Debugging with Visual Studio:** Set breakpoints, step through code, and inspect variables.
- **Logging:** Use `Console.WriteLine` or logging frameworks for debugging output.

Common Issues and Solutions

- **Component Rendering Issues:**
  a. Check data binding correctness.
  b. Verify component lifecycle methods.
  c. Inspect component hierarchy for potential conflicts.
- **JavaScript Interop Errors:**
  a. Ensure correct parameter types and return values.
  b. Handle exceptions properly.
  c. Use try-catch blocks to protect against errors.
- **Performance Issues:**
  a. Profile your application to identify bottlenecks.
  b. Optimize component rendering and state management.
  c. Reduce JavaScript interop.
- **Deployment Issues:**
  a. Verify server configuration and deployment scripts.
  b. Check network connectivity and firewall rules.

c. Inspect browser console for errors.

Debugging Code Example

```csharp
C#
@code {
    private int count = 0;

    private void IncrementCount()
    {
        try
        {
            count++;
        }
        catch (Exception ex)
        {
            Console.Error.WriteLine($"Error incrementing count: {ex}");
        }
    }
}
```

224

Troubleshooting Tips

- **Isolate the issue:** Break down the problem into smaller components.
- **Use the debugger effectively:** Step through code to understand execution flow.
- **Inspect the DOM:** Check for unexpected changes in the UI.
- **Review network traffic:** Look for failed requests or slow responses.
- **Check browser console:** Look for error messages or warnings.
- **Search for similar issues:** Online communities and forums can be helpful.

Additional Considerations

- **Logging:** Use a structured logging framework for detailed logs.

225

- **Remote debugging:** Debug production issues using remote debugging tools.
- **Performance profiling:** Identify performance bottlenecks and optimize accordingly.
- **Error handling:** Implement robust error handling mechanisms.
- **User testing:** Gather feedback from users to identify issues.

By following these guidelines and utilizing available tools, you can effectively debug and troubleshoot your Blazor WebAssembly applications.

Would you like to delve deeper into a specific debugging technique or explore common error scenarios?

Chapter 14:

Exploring the Blazor Documentation and Learning Resources

Exploring the Blazor Documentation and Learning Resources

Unlocking the Power of Blazor: A Deep Dive into Documentation and Resources

Blazor, a framework for building interactive web UIs using C#, offers a rich ecosystem of documentation and learning resources. Effectively navigating these materials is crucial for mastering the framework.

Official Blazor Documentation

The official Blazor documentation is the primary source of information. It provides comprehensive coverage of all aspects of Blazor development:

- **Core concepts:** Understand the fundamental building blocks of Blazor, including components, data binding, routing, and dependency injection.
- **Tutorials:** Follow step-by-step guides to build your first Blazor application and learn core concepts through practical examples.
- **API reference:** Explore the details of classes, methods, and properties used in Blazor development.
- **Samples:** Dive into code examples to understand how different features are implemented.

Leveraging Online Communities

The Blazor community is vibrant and offers valuable insights:

- **Stack Overflow:** A vast repository of questions and answers on various programming topics, including Blazor.
- **Blazor Discord:** Join the official Discord server for real-time discussions and support.
- **Blazor Reddit:** Engage in discussions and share knowledge with other Blazor developers.
- **Blazor Forums:** Participate in dedicated Blazor forums for in-depth conversations.

Third-Party Learning Resources

Complement your learning with external resources:

- **Online courses:** Platforms like Pluralsight, Udemy, and LinkedIn Learning offer structured Blazor courses.
- **Video tutorials:** YouTube provides a wealth of free tutorials on Blazor.
- **Books:** Explore dedicated Blazor books for in-depth coverage.

- **Blogs and articles:** Stay updated with the latest trends and best practices through developer blogs.

Building a Strong Foundation

To maximize your learning experience:

- **Master C#:** A strong foundation in C# is essential for effective Blazor development.
- **Understand web development fundamentals:** HTML, CSS, and JavaScript knowledge are beneficial.
- **Practice regularly:** Build small projects to solidify your skills.
- **Contribute to open-source:** Engage with the community by contributing to Blazor projects.
- **Stay updated:** Keep up with the latest Blazor developments and best practices.

Effective Learning Strategies

230

- **Start with the basics:** Grasp core concepts before diving into advanced topics.
- **Experiment and explore:** Try different approaches and learn from mistakes.
- **Build projects:** Apply your knowledge to real-world projects to solidify learning.
- **Join online communities:** Engage with other developers to share knowledge and get help.
- **Seek mentorship:** Find experienced developers to guide your learning.

Recommended Learning Path

1. Master C# fundamentals.
2. Start with the official Blazor documentation to grasp core concepts.
3. Build small projects to practice what you've learned.
4. Explore online tutorials and courses for in-depth knowledge.

5. Join the Blazor community to learn from others and contribute.
6. Continue learning and experimenting with new features.

By following these guidelines and leveraging the available resources, you can become proficient in Blazor development and build exceptional web applications.

Would you like to delve deeper into a specific learning resource or explore advanced learning strategies?

Conclusion

Conclusion: Mastering Blazor WebAssembly

Blazor WebAssembly has emerged as a powerful tool for building interactive web applications using C#. By understanding its core concepts, best practices, and advanced techniques, developers can create robust, performant, and user-friendly applications.

Key Takeaways

- **Component-based architecture:** Build reusable UI elements for efficient development.
- **Data binding:** Seamlessly connect C# code to the UI for dynamic updates.
- **Routing:** Create navigation experiences within your application.
- **Dependency injection:** Manage dependencies effectively for maintainability.
- **State management:** Handle complex application state efficiently.

- **Data fetching:** Integrate with APIs to retrieve and display data.
- **Styling:** Create visually appealing UIs using CSS and frameworks.
- **User interactions:** Handle user input and events effectively.
- **Performance optimization:** Improve application speed and responsiveness.
- **Deployment:** Choose the right deployment strategy for your application.

Building on Your Foundation

To further enhance your Blazor skills, consider exploring these areas:

- **Blazor Hybrid:** Combine the best of Blazor WebAssembly and Blazor Server.
- **WebAssembly interop:** Access low-level browser APIs.
- **Server-side Blazor:** Explore the server-side rendering capabilities of Blazor.

- **Advanced debugging techniques:** Utilize browser developer tools and debugging features effectively.
- **Accessibility:** Ensure your applications are accessible to users with disabilities.
- **Security:** Implement robust security measures to protect your application and user data.

The Future of Blazor

Blazor is a rapidly evolving framework with a promising future. Stay updated on the latest features and best practices to leverage its full potential.

Code Example: Combining Key Concepts

```
C#

@page "/counter"

<h3>Counter</h3>
<p>Current count: @currentCount</p>
```

235

```
<button class="btn btn-primary"
@onclick="IncrementCount">Click me</button>

@code {

    private int currentCount







    = 0;


    private void IncrementCount()
    {

        currentCount++;



```

// Imagine saving count to local storage or a
database here

}

}

This simple counter component demonstrates core
concepts like data binding, event handling, and potential
data persistence.

By mastering Blazor WebAssembly, you can create
exceptional web applications that deliver outstanding
user experiences. Continuous learning and
experimentation are key to staying ahead in this dynamic
field.

Appendix

Appendix: Glossary of Terms

Core Blazor Terms

- **Component:** A reusable building block of a Blazor UI, combining HTML, CSS, and C# code.
- **Razor Syntax:** A syntax for embedding C# code within HTML templates
- **Data Binding:** A mechanism for synchronizing data between the UI and C# code.
- **Lifecycle Methods:** Methods invoked at different stages of a component's life.
- **Routing:** The process of navigating between different pages or views in a Blazor app.
- **Dependency Injection:** A design pattern for providing dependencies to components.

Additional Terms

- **State Management:** The process of managing application data and its flow.
- **Event Handling:** The process of responding to user interactions.
- **Cascading Parameters:** Passing data down through component hierarchies.

- **Event Bubbling:** The propagation of events up the component hierarchy.
- **Scoped CSS:** CSS styles that are isolated to a specific component.
- **Blazor WebAssembly:** A client-side web UI framework using C# and WebAssembly.
- **Blazor Server:** A server-side hosting model for Blazor applications. *IndexedDB: A browser API for storing structured data.
- **Authentication:** Verifying a user's identity.
- **Authorization:** Determining what a user can do after authentication.
- **Deployment:** The process of making a Blazor application available to users.

Abbreviations

- **UI:** User Interface
- **HTTP:** Hypertext Transfer Protocol
- **JSON:** JavaScript Object Notation
- **CSS:** Cascading Style Sheets

- **HTML:** HyperText Markup Language
- **C#:** C Sharp
- **DI:** Dependency Injection

This glossary provides a comprehensive overview of key terms used in Blazor development. Understanding these terms is essential for effectively building Blazor applications.

A: Glossary of Terms

A: Glossary of Terms

Core Blazor Terms

- **Component:** A reusable building block of a Blazor UI, combining HTML, CSS, and C# code.
- **Razor Syntax:** A syntax for embedding C# code within HTML templates.
- **Data Binding:** A mechanism for synchronizing data between the UI and C# code.

- **Lifecycle Methods:** Methods invoked at different stages of a component's life.
- **Routing:** The process of navigating between different pages or views in a Blazor app.
- **Dependency Injection:** A design pattern for providing dependencies to components.
- **State Management:** The process of managing application data and its flow.
- **Event Handling:** The process of responding to user interactions.
- **Cascading Parameters:** Passing data down through component hierarchies.
- **Event Bubbling:** The propagation of events up the component hierarchy.
- **Scoped CSS:** CSS styles that are isolated to a specific component.
- **Blazor WebAssembly:** A client-side web UI framework using C# and WebAssembly.
- **Blazor Server:** A server-side hosting model for Blazor applications.
- **IndexedDB:** A browser API for storing structured data.

- **Authentication:** Verifying a user's identity.
- **Authorization:** Determining what a user can do after authentication.
- **Deployment:** The process of making a Blazor application available to users.

Additional Terms

- **Component-Level Styling:** Applying CSS styles to a specific component.
- **Global Styling:** Applying CSS styles to the entire application.
- **HTTP:** Hypertext Transfer Protocol
- **JSON:** JavaScript Object Notation
- **CSS:** Cascading Style Sheets
- **HTML:** HyperText Markup Language
- **C#:** C Sharp
- **DI:** Dependency Injection
- **UI:** User Interface
- **PWA:** Progressive Web App

Note: This glossary provides a foundational understanding of key Blazor terms. For more in-depth definitions and explanations, refer to the main content of this guide.

Made in the USA
Columbia, SC
21 November 2024

47209489R00135